Free time

Leisure activities

1 **Read. Then match.**

1 surfing   a the guitar

2 reading   b the internet

3 playing   c online

4 walking   d magazines

5 chatting   e the dog

T0344329

2 **Find four more activities.**

decleaningbaskiingerskateboardingmoskippingsicookinged

3 **Write *a*, *e*, *i* or *o*. Then number.**

 a

 b

 c

 d

 e

 f

1 pl a y i ng
  h o ck e y

2 p _ _ nt _ ng

3 sk _ pp _ ng

4 w _ tch _ ng
  f _ lms

5 c _ _ k _ ng

6 r _ _ d _ ng
  m _ g _ z _ n _ s

1 She doesn't like playing the guitar

4 Look. Then match and write.

1

a _____ reading magazines.

2

b _____ skateboarding.

3

c <u>She doesn't like</u> cooking.

4

d _____ playing computer games.

5

e _____ skiing.

6

f _____ playing the guitar.

7

g _____ watching TV.

5 Unscramble the questions and answers.

1 Tom / what / doing / does / like

Q: <u>What does Tom like doing?</u>

computer games / likes / playing / he

A: _____

2 what / Mum and Dad / like / doing / do

Q: _____

reading / they / like / magazines

A: _____

3 like / doing / Mary / what / does

Q: _____

likes / cooking / she

A: _____

6 Read. Then circle.

1 (*Do / Does*) Sara like cooking? Yes, she does.

2 Does Tom like painting? No, he (*don't / doesn't*).

3 Do they (*like / likes*) walking the dog? Yes, they do.

4 (*Do / Does*) you like skateboarding? Yes, I do.

5 Does she (*like / likes*) skipping? Yes, she does.

6 Do you like watching TV? Yes, I (*do / does*).

1 Does Sara like playing hockey?

7 Write.

1 (*Tom / read / magazines / ✘*)

Tom doesn't like reading magazines.

2 (*Sara / play / hockey / ?*)

_____

3 (*Sara / chat / online / ✔*)

_____

4 (*they / play / computer games / ✔*)

_____

5 (*we / watch / films / ✘*)

_____

8 Find and write two questions. Then write answers.

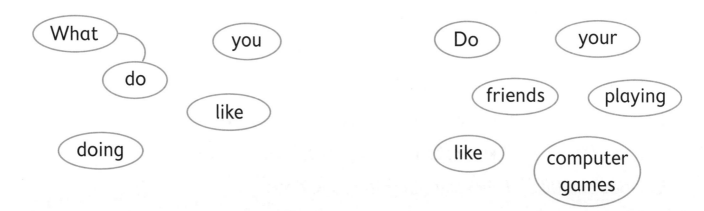

1 Q: _____

A: _____

2 Q: _____

A: _____

9 Read. Who likes sports?

_____ likes sports.

Hi! My name's Kate and I'm 9 years old. I'm from Ireland. I like watching TV and playing computer games. *Farm* is my favourite computer game. It's really cool! I also like singing and dancing with my friends at parties. My friends think I'm a very good dancer. I don't like cleaning and I don't like cooking. My sister and my mum like cooking. I don't like cooking, but I like eating!

Hello! I'm Santiago and I'm from Argentina. I'm 10 years old. I like playing football in the park with my friends. I also like skateboarding and skiing. Sports are great! I like reading sports magazines, too. My brother doesn't like sports. He likes watching TV and surfing the internet. I don't like watching TV and I don't like surfing the internet. They're boring!

10 Read again. Then circle _T_ (True) or _F_ (False).

1 Kate is from Argentina.   T / F

2 She likes playing computer games.   T / F

3 She doesn't like dancing.   T / F

4 Kate's sister likes cooking.   T / F

5 Santiago is 10.   T / F

6 He doesn't like skiing.   T / F

7 He likes watching TV.   T / F

8 Santiago's brother likes surfing the internet.   T / F

1 Describing likes and dislikes

11 Write three things you like doing and three things you don't like doing.

I like ...	I don't like ...

12 Write about the things you like and don't like doing.
Then write about a friend.

_Me_

My name is _____
and I'm _____ years old.
I like _____
_____
_____
_____
_____
_____

My friend

My friend's name is
_____ and
he/she is _____ years old.
_____ likes _____
_____
_____
_____
_____

Wild animals

Wild animals, habitats

1 Look and match.

1 elephant   **2** crab

3 gorilla   **4** lion

5 monkey   **6** zebra

2 Write. Use words from the box.

camel   crocodile   giraffe   hippo   panda   ~~tiger~~

1 I've got orange and black stripes.   tiger

2 I'm tall and I eat leaves.   _____

3 I live in rivers and I've got a long tail.   _____

4 I live in deserts and I walk slowly.   _____

5 I'm big and grey and I like water.   _____

6 I'm black and white and I live in forests.   _____

3 Match the two parts of the words.

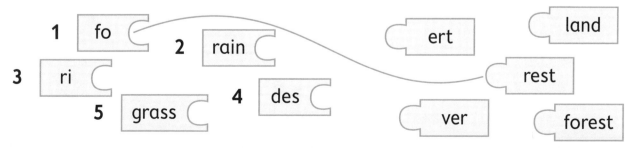

1 fo   ert   land

2 rain

3 ri   rest

4 des

5 grass   ver   forest

4 Read. Then circle.

Orangutans (*live* / *lives*) in the rainforest. They (*have* / *are*) herbivores.
They (*eat* / *eating*) a lot of fruit. They've (*are* / *got*) very long arms and
they (*likes* / *like*) climbing trees.

5 Read and underline the mistakes. Then write.

1	Does lions eat meat?	Do lions eat meat?
2	They eats fruit.	
3	Do elephants lives in forests?	
4	Yes, they does.	
5	Does hippos eat fruit?	
6	Giraffes eating leaves.	

**6 Draw your favourite animal. Then write about what it eats
and where it lives.**

7 **Read and complete. Use words from the box.**

What	do	does	eat	lives	eats	live	Where

1 Where ___do___ giraffes live? They _____ in Africa.

2 _____ do monkeys live? They _____ in forests.

3 What _____ gorillas eat? They _____ fruit and leaves.

4 _____ do pandas eat? They _____ bamboo.

8 **Read. Then unscramble and write.**

1

animal / what's / favourite / your

What's your favourite animal?

My favourite animal is the crocodile.

2

live / where / crocodiles / do

_____

_____

They live in rivers.

3

what / they / eat / do

_____

_____

They eat fish and meat.

9 **Read and match.**

1	Giraffes eat		**a**	swim quickly.
2	Crocodiles		**b**	a lot of leaves.
3	Giraffes can run fast		**c**	65 teeth.
4	Crocodiles have got		**d**	but they walk slowly.

10 **Read. Then circle.**

1 (*How much* / *How many*) teeth have pandas got?

They've got (*much* / *a lot*) – 42!

2 (*How much* / *How many*) meat do crocodiles eat?

They eat (*much* / *a lot*).

3 (*How much* / *How many*) types of elephant are there?

(*There's* / *There are*) two types: African and Asian.

11 **Read and complete. Use words from the box.**

fast slowly ~~well~~ climb walk swim

1 Crocodiles swim __well__ .   2 Camels run _____ .

3 Elephants _____ slowly.   4 Monkeys _____ well.

4 Fish _____ fast.   6 Giraffes walk _____ but run fast.

12 Read. Then circle.

Tigers

Tigers are very big cats. They live in the jungle and they eat meat. They're big and strong. They've got black and orange stripes, sharp teeth and sharp claws. They can run very fast and they can swim well. They like water and they often swim when it's hot. There aren't any tigers in my country but there's a zoo near my house. It's got three big tigers and some tiger cubs, too. They're amazing!

Zebras

Zebras live in grasslands in Africa. They look like horses and they've got black and white stripes. Zebras are herbivores: they eat grass, leaves and fruit. They eat during the day and sleep at night. Zebras can hear very well and they can also see well at night. They can run fast, too. Baby zebras are amazing. They can walk when they are only 20 minutes old! And they can run when they are 1 hour old!

1 Tigers live in (*grasslands* / *the jungle*).

2 They (*can* / *can't*) run fast.

3 They (*like* / *don't like*) water.

4 Zebras are (*carnivores* / *herbivores*).

5 They (*eat* / *sleep*) at night.

13 Read again. Then answer.

1 What do tigers eat?   They eat meat.

2 Can they swim well?   _____

3 Where do zebras live?   _____

4 What do they eat?   _____

5 Can they hear well?   _____

2 Describing animals

Remember!

Add -s to most plural nouns.

pandas lions monkeys tigers crocodiles

14 Think of two animals. Write notes.

Animal:		Animal:	
lives:		lives:	
eats:		eats:	
has got:		has got:	
can:		can:	
can't:		can't:	

15 Write about the animals from Activity 14.

The seasons

3

Seasons, weather, seasonal activities

1 **Unscramble. Find the seasons.**

1 inetrw   w i n t e r   2 auumtn   _ _ _ _ _ _

3 srpign   _ _ _ _ _ _   4 rsemum   _ _ _ _ _ _

2 **Match the two parts of the words.**

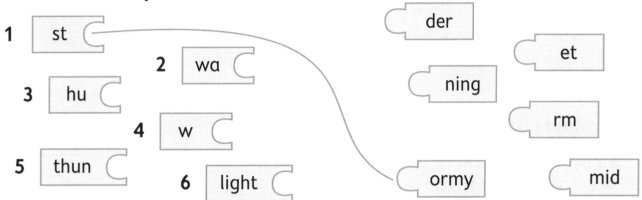

1 st   der

2 wa   et

3 hu   ning

4 w   rm

5 thun   ormy

6 light   mid

3 **Write *a*, *e*, *i* or *o*.**

1 gO wAtEr skiing

2 g _ c _ mp _ ng

3 g _ sn _ wb _ _ _ rd _ ng

4 g _ h _ k _ ng

4 Read. Then match.

1

What's the weather like in spring?

a

Sometimes it's wet and there's thunder and lightning. Other times it's warm.

2

What's the weather like in winter?

b

It's hot and sunny. Sometimes it's humid.

3

What's the weather like in summer?

c

It's cold and snowy.

5 Unscramble and write. Then draw.

1 windy / today / it's

It's windy today.

2 thunder / there's / and / lightning

_____

3 the / temperature / what's / today

_____

4 today / 17 / degrees / it's

_____

6 Look and read. Then write.

	skiing	hiking	camping	surfing	cycling
spring	Ben	Ben	Ben	Tom	Tom
summer		Jo and Sue	Jo and Sue	Tom	Kim and Mark
autumn		Kim and Mark	Tom		Ben
winter	Ben				

1 <u>Ben goes skiing in winter and spring.</u> (*Ben / skiing*)

2 _____ (*Kim and Mark / hiking*)

3 _____ (*Tom / surfing*)

4 _____ (*Jo and Sue / camping*)

5 _____ (*Ben / cycling*)

6 _____ (*Tom / camping*)

7 Write about what you do in each season.

1 _____ (*spring*)

2 _____ (*summer*)

3 _____ (*autumn*)

4 _____ (*winter*)

What was the weather like?

8 Complete the sentences with *is* or *was*.

1 What 's the temperature today?

2 What _____ the weather like yesterday?

3 It _____ sunny and warm today.

4 It _____ 25 degrees yesterday.

5 What _____ the weather like last winter?

6 It _____ 15 degrees today!

9 What was the weather like last winter? Look and write.

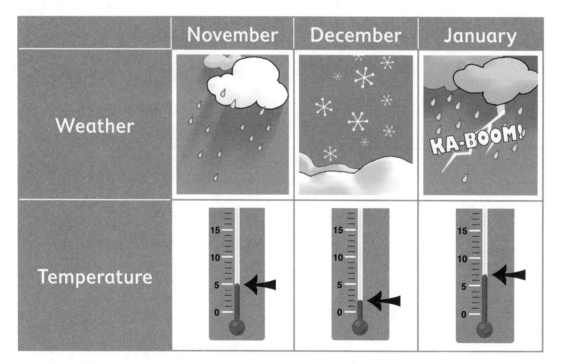

	November	December	January
Weather			
Temperature			

1 <u>What was the weather like in November?</u> It was rainy.

2 _____ It was 5 degrees.

3 _____ It was stormy.

4 _____ It was 2 degrees.

5 _____ It was 7 degrees.

6 _____ It was snowy.

10 **What's the weather like today where you live? Write.**

_____

11 **Read. Then write the temperatures.**

Good morning! Here is today's weather.

Here in the north it's cloudy with some rain and a temperature of 21 degrees. In the west it's very hot and humid. The temperature is 35 degrees! Now let's look at the south. There is a hurricane. It isn't cold. The temperature is 24 degrees. And now the east: there's a lot of rain and wind. The temperature is 20 degrees. Don't forget your umbrella!

1 north: _____twenty-one_____ degrees

2 west: _____ degrees

3 south: _____ degrees

4 east: _____ degrees

12 **Read again. Then circle _T_ (True) or _F_ (False).**

1 It's sunny in the north.   T / (F)

2 It's wet and windy in the west.   T / F

3 There's thunder and lightning in the west.   T / F

4 There's a hurricane in the south.   T / F

5 It's rainy in the east.   T / F

3 A weather report

13 What can you do? Write two activities for each season.

1 autumn: _____

2 winter: _____

3 spring: _____

4 summer: _____

14 Look at page 17 again. Then write about the weather where you live.

- What's the weather like today?

- What's the temperature today?

- What activities can / can't you do?

_____

_____

_____

_____

_____

_____

_____

_____

_____

My week

Activities, time

1 Complete the sentences with *have*, *do*, *practise* or *study*.

1 She ____has____ ballet lessons.

2 You _____ karate.

3 We _____ English.

4 I _____ the piano.

5 You _____ gymnastics.

6 I _____ Maths.

7 We _____ the violin.

8 He _____ music lessons.

2 Write. Use words from Activity 1.

1

2

3

She has ballet lessons.

4

5

6

3 Draw the time.

1

It's half past three.

2

It's quarter past twelve.

3

It's nine o'clock.

4

It's quarter to seven.

4 Complete. Then match and write the letter.

| they | practise | have | does | ~~do~~ | he |

1 What ___do___ you do on Sundays? |d|

2 What do _____ do on Mondays? | |

3 What does _____ do on Wednesdays? | |

4 Does she always _____ music lessons on Thursdays? | |

5 Does your friend always _____ the piano on Sundays? | |

6 What _____ she do on Fridays? | |

a She learns to cook.

b Yes, she does.

c No, he doesn't.

d I learn to draw.

e He does gymnastics.

f They do karate.

5 Answer about you.

1 What do you do on Sundays?

_____

2 Do you always study English on Mondays?

_____

6 Read the letter. Then circle.

Hi Jamie,

How are you? I've got a new timetable this year.
I (*has* / *have*) piano lessons on Wednesdays at half
(*past* / *to*) three. I (*do* / *does*) my homework every
day at four o'clock. On Thursdays I do karate, and
my sister (*practise* / *practises*) the violin and
(*learns* / *learn*) to draw. On Fridays I play
basketball after school.

What's your timetable like this year?
When (*do* / *does*) you have music lessons?
Write soon.
Liam.

7 Read again. Then write questions.

1 When does Liam have piano lessons?
   He has piano lessons on Wednesdays at half past three.

2 When does he do homework?

_____

8 Read again. Then write questions.

1 _____

She practises the violin and learns to draw on Thursdays.

2 _____

He plays basketball on Fridays after school.

4 always, often, never

9 **Look and write sentences about Jo. Use *always*, *never* and *often*.**

	Do homework		Learn to cook		Study English		Have music lessons	
	Jo	Me	Jo	Me	Jo	Me	Jo	Me
Mon	✔				✔			
Tues	✔		✔					
Wed	✔		✔		✔			
Thurs	✔		✔					
Fri	✔		✔		✔			
Sat	✔				✔			
Sun	✔							

1 <u>Jo always does her homework.</u>　(*do homework*)

2 _____　(*have music lessons*)

3 _____　(*learn to cook*)

4 _____　(*study English*)

10 **Look at Activity 9 and complete the table about you. Then write sentences with *always*, *never* and *often*.**

1 _____　(*do homework*)

2 _____　(*have music lessons*)

3 _____　(*learn to cook*)

4 _____　(*study English*)

11 Look at Rosa's timetable. Then circle _T_ (True) or _F_ (False)

	Morning	Afternoon
MON	study English (9.15—11.30)	practise the piano (2.15—3.15)
TUES	study English (9.15—11.30)	have ballet lessons (4.00—5.00)
WED	study English (9.15—11.30)	practise the piano (2.30—3.30)
THURS	study English (9.15—11.30)	have ballet lessons (2.45—3.45)
FRI	study English (9.15—11.30)	do gymnastics (3.00—4.00)
SAT	do karate (10.00—11.00)	practise the piano (3.15—4.00)

1 On Mondays Rosa practises the piano at half past two.   T / F

2 On Tuesdays she has a ballet lesson at four o'clock.   T / F

3 On Wednesdays she practises the piano at quarter to two.   T / F

4 On Thursdays she studies Maths in the morning.   T / F

5 On Fridays she does gymnastics at three o'clock.   T / F

6 On Saturdays she does karate in the afternoon.   T / F

12 Look at Activity 11 again. Correct the false statements.

1 On Mondays Rosa practises the piano at quarter past two.

2 True.

3 _____

4 _____

5 _____

6 _____

Remember!

2.45 = quarter **to** three   3.15 = quarter **past** three

13 Make your own timetable.

	Morning	Afternoon
MON		
TUES		
WED		
THURS		
FRI		
SAT		

14 Look at Activity 6 on page 21 and write about your week.

On Mondays I _____

_____

_____

_____

_____

_____

_____

1 Write. Use words from the box.

| astronaut | ballet dancer | singer | journalist | lawyer | police officer |

1 _____

2 _____

3 _____

4 _____

5 _____

6 _____

2 Unscramble. Then write.

1 pcotmuer romgrapmer   c o m p u t e r   p r o g r a m m e r

2 rfmare   _ _ _ _ _ _

3 firifergthe   _ _ _ _ _ _ _ _ _ _ _

4 fmli satr   _ _ _ _   _ _ _ _

3 Write the jobs. What's the secret word? _____

1 I fix cars.

2 I take photos.

3 I build houses.

4 I work with wood.

5 I train and listen to my coach.

			1	m	e	c	h	a	n	i	c
2	p		o		o		r			e	
3		u					r				
4			r			n					
5	a						e				

4 Unscramble the sentences. Then match.

1 to / player / be / basketball / I / a / want

<u>I want to be a basketball player.</u>

a

_____

2 don't / police / to / want / officer / be / I / a

b

_____

_____

3 astronaut / be / want / don't / to / an / I

c

_____

_____

4 a / want / film / to / star / be / I

d

_____

_____

5 Write the questions.

1 <u>What does she want to be?</u>

She wants to be a builder.

2 _____

I want to be a ballet dancer.

3 _____

He wants to be a lawyer.

6 Read. Then match.

1 Mary likes writing.   **a** nurse

2 Pete likes running.   **b** journalist

3 James likes helping people.   **c** film stars

4 Roger likes working on cars.   **d** ballet dancers

5 Sarah and Kim like dancing.   **e** carpenter

6 Tim and John like acting.   **f** mechanic

7 Julie likes making things.   **g** athlete

7 Look at Activity 6 again. Write questions and answers.

1 _____Does_____ Mary _____want to be_____ an athlete?
No, she doesn't. She wants to be a journalist.

2 _____ Pete _____ an athlete?

_____

3 _____ James _____ a nurse?

_____

4 _____ Roger _____ a carpenter?

_____

5 _____ Sarah and Kim _____ ballet dancers?

_____

6 _____ Tim and John _____ journalists?

_____

7 _____ Julie _____ a carpenter?

_____

I want to be a singer because I like singing

8 Read and complete. Use words from the box.

~~want~~   be   like   can   like   because   practise   because

Ben

I ¹$\underline{want}$ to be a journalist ²_____ I like talking to people and asking questions! I also ³_____ reading magazines and I ⁴_____ writing stories every day.

Sue

I want to ⁵_____ a builder ⁶_____ I like making things. I ⁷_____ drawing houses and bridges and I ⁸_____ do Maths.

9 Read. Then circle.

1 Why does Wendy (*want* / *wants*) to be a doctor? Because she likes (*help* / *helping*) people.

2 Why (*do* / *does*) he want to be a singer? Because he (*likes* / *can*) sing.

3 Why do (*you* / *he*) want to be a farmer? Because I (*like* / *likes*) vegetables.

4 (*What* / *Why*) do they want to be film stars? Because they (*like* / *likes*) acting.

10 What do you want to be? Why? Write.

_____

_____

11 Read. Then answer.

Dear Uncle Rob,

Can you help me? At school we are doing a project on jobs.
We choose a job we want to do and ask someone about it.

I want to be an athlete so I want to find out what an athlete does.
I want to know what time an athlete gets up in the morning and starts
work. Are athletes brave? Can I come to watch you run one morning
next week and talk to your coach? I've got a lot of questions to ask!

Thank you, Jason

1 Who is Jason writing to?

<u>He's writing to his Uncle Rob.</u>

2 Why is he writing the email?

_____

3 What's his school project about?

_____

4 What does Jason want to be?

_____

5 When does he want to watch his uncle run?

_____

Remember!

| I/you/we/they: like | but | he/she/it: like**s** |
| Do I/you/we/they like ...? | but | **Does** he/she/it like ...? |

12 Read. Then match.

1 Dear

2 I want to be

3 Can I

4 What time do

a you get up?

b visit your farm?

c Aunt Kate,

d a farmer.

13 Look at Activity 11 on page 29. Imagine you are doing the same project. Then write an email to ask someone for help.

- Who are you writing to?
- What do you want to know?
- What job do you want to ask about?
- Where do you want to go? When?

In the rainforest

Nature, prepositions

6

1 Write. Use words from the box.

| bridge | hut | lake | nest | vines | waterfall |

1 _____

2 _____

3 _____

4 _____

5 _____

6 _____

2 Match.

1 through
2 across
3 towards
4 around

a

b

c

d

3 Read. Then circle.

1 a bird with a long tail and colourful feathers: (*tapir* / *parrot*)

2 a very big, scary spider: (*hummingbird* / *giant tarantula*)

3 an animal with a short neck and big ears: (*tapir* / *parrot*)

4 a very small bird: (*hummingbird* / *parrot*)

6 The hut is near the river

4 Unscramble the sentences. Then write.

1 two mountains / there / behind / the rainforest / are

There are two mountains behind the rainforest.

2 a waterfall / between / the mountains / there's

3 a river / there's / the rainforest / near

4 a bridge / across / there's / the river

5 huts / near / there / are / the bridge

5 Read your answers in Activity 4. Then draw the picture.

6 Look and read. Then write questions and answers.

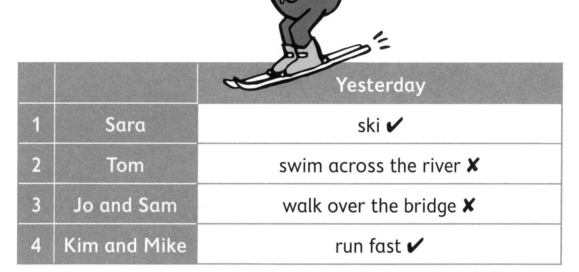

		Yesterday
1	Sara	ski ✔
2	Tom	swim across the river ✗
3	Jo and Sam	walk over the bridge ✗
4	Kim and Mike	run fast ✔

1 <u>Could Tom ski yesterday?</u>   <u>No, he couldn't.</u>

2 _____   _____

3 _____   _____

4 _____   _____

7 Complete about you. Then write.

Yesterday	
	✗
	✔

Yesterday _____

_____ .

6 walk / walked

8 Read. Then circle.

1 I (*walk* / (*walked*)) to the shop yesterday.

2 They could (*climb* / *climbed*) trees when they were young.

3 She always (*plays* / *played*) football after school.

4 They (*hike* / *hiked*) last autumn.

5 Yesterday I (*watch* / *watched*) TV.

6 She (*practises* / *practised*) the piano every day at four o'clock.

9 Read. Then complete.

Last year I ¹visited (*visit*) the New Forest. We ²_____

(*camp*) in the forest. The weather ³_____ (*be*) nice and we

⁴_____ (*walk*) every day.

The New Forest has got a lot of horses. We ⁵_____ (*can go*)

near them but we ⁶_____ (*cannot give*) them food.

There ⁷_____ (*be*) also a lot of trees and some small

lakes. We ⁸_____ (*can walk*) around a big lake that

⁹_____ (*be*) near our campsite. The campsite was great.

Our trip ¹⁰_____ (*be*) such fun!

10 Write about your last summer holiday.

_____

_____

_____

11 Read. Then circle _T_ (True) or _F_ (False).

THE AMAZON RAINFOREST

The Amazon Rainforest is the largest rainforest in the world. It's in South America. More than half of the rainforest is in Brazil. It takes its name from the river that runs through it: the Amazon River. The Amazon is the second longest river in the world.

It's called a rainforest because it rains a lot! It rains every day, usually in the afternoon. In the Amazon the rainy season is between December and May. The dry season is from June until November but there's still rain!

There are a lot of plants and animals in the Amazon Rainforest. Scientists use some of the plants for medicines, to keep us healthy. The Amazon Rainforest is a very important! We must protect it!

1	The Amazon Rainforest is in South Africa.	T / F
2	It takes its name from a river.	T / F
3	The Amazon River is the longest river in the world.	T / F
4	It doesn't rain very often in the Amazon Rainforest.	T / F
5	The rainy season starts in June.	T / F
6	There's still rain in the dry season.	T / F
7	A lot of animals live in the rainforest.	T / F

6 An article

Remember!

We use **capital letters** for the names of countries, cities, rivers and mountains.

South **A**frica   **L**ondon   **A**mazon **R**iver   **M**ount **E**verest

12 **Think of a place in your country. Write notes.**

Name of place:	
Where it is:	
Things to see:	
Things to do:	
Other information:	

13 **Write an article about the place from Activity 12.**

_____

_____

_____

_____

_____

_____

_____

Feelings

Emotions

1 Find and circle. Then write.

O	D	Y	A	W	N	I	N	G
S	H	Z	L	V	N	G	S	M
S	H	O	U	T	I	N	G	S
C	R	Y	I	N	G	T	R	M
U	S	G	F	I	G	P	V	I
E	T	F	G	C	I	I	L	L
S	Q	D	S	K	O	P	N	I
O	P	Y	N	T	O	I	X	N
J	S	H	A	K	I	N	G	G

1 I'm _____smiling_____ because I'm happy.

2 I'm _____ because I'm scared.

3 I'm _____ because I'm tired.

4 I'm _____ because I'm sad.

5 I'm _____ because they can't hear me.

2 Unscramble and write. Then number.

a

b

c

d

e

1 smabrarsdee   e m b a r r a s s e d

2 poudr   _ _ _ _ _

3 noevrsu   _ _ _ _ _ _ _

4 raexdle   _ _ _ _ _ _ _

5 ereielvd   _ _ _ _ _ _ _ _

3 **Read. Then match and write the letter.**

1 Why are you crying? $\boxed{d}$

    a Because there's a funny movie on TV.

2 Why are you nervous? $\boxed{}$

    b Because my grandad can't hear her!

3 Why are you laughing? $\boxed{}$

    c Because she's embarrassed.

4 Why is your sister shouting? $\boxed{}$

    d Because I'm sad.

5 Why is your mum blushing? $\boxed{}$

    e Because I have a piano test.

6 Why are you tired? $\boxed{}$

    f Because I walked to school.

4 **Unscramble the questions and answers.**

1 she / smiling / why / is

    Q: Why is she smiling? _____

smiling / she's / because / birthday / it's / her

    A: She's smiling because it's her birthday. _____

2 your / crying / why / is / brother

    Q: _____

because / he's / crying / he's / hurt

    A: _____

3 are / shaking / you / why

    Q: _____

scared / I'm / because / I'm / shaking

    A: _____

5 Answer the questions.

1 What makes you feel embarrassed?
<u>Singing makes me feel embarrassed.</u> (*sing*)

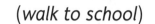

2 What makes you feel tired?

_____ (*walk to school*)

3 What makes you feel relieved?

_____ (*pass a test*)

4 What makes you feel proud?

_____ (*play football well*)

6 Write the questions. Use the words from the box.

> What's the matter?   Why are you crying?   ~~How do you feel?~~

1 <u>How do you feel?</u>_____ I feel embarrassed.

2 _____ I'm sad.

3 _____ I feel tired.

7 Read. Then complete.

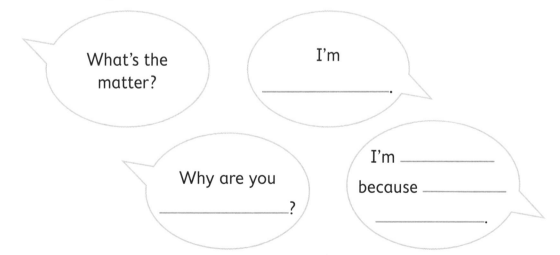

What's the matter?

I'm _____.

Why are you _____?

I'm _____ because _____ _____.

7 me, him, her, them, us

8 **Read. Then circle.**

> Dear Mum,
>
> (*I* / *Me*) am having a great time with Aunt Sue and Uncle John.
>
> Aunt Sue gives (*I* / *me*) a lot of jobs to do. They're fun jobs so it's OK. Uncle John is very funny. (*He* / *Him*) tells (*we* / *us*) funny stories about when (*he* / *him*) was a boy. They make me laugh.
>
> Yesterday (*we* / *us*) visited a park and played football. It was so much fun.
>
> Aunt Sue and Uncle John are terrific. I love staying with (*they* / *them*).
>
> Sarah

9 **Match. Then write.**

1 We don't understand.

2 The cat is thirsty.

3 It's his birthday.

4 Pick up the towels.

a Let's give _____ a cake.

b Put _____ in the cupboard.

c Give _____ some water.

d Can you help, _____us_____?

10 **Unscramble and write. Then circle *T* (True) or *F* (False) about you.**

1 teacher / hand out / my / me / books / the / asks / never / to

My teacher never asks me to hand out the books.   *T / F*

2 mum / gives / birthday / always / books / me / my / for / my

_____   *T / F*

3 granny / my / often / us / tells / stories / interesting

_____   *T / F*

11 Read. Does the writer like *Feelings*? Why?

Feelings: A school musical

Feelings is the new play from Kidstown Primary School. And it's fantastic! It starts when a group of children go on a journey. They want to go by plane but things go wrong and they go to a train station! They miss the plane and instead they go by train, boat and car!

It's a fun story and it can make you feel a lot of different things. There are times when the children are worried and others when they are angry.

There are other moments when everyone is happy and excited. There are also one or two moments when the children are sad.

When you are watching, you may ask yourself, 'Why am I smiling?' or 'Why am I crying or laughing so much?' This play is funny and has a little bit of everything! You really must go and see it.

12 Read again. Then circle.

1 *Feelings* is a (*film* / *play*).

2 The story is about (*a group of children* / *Kidstown Primary School*).

3 The children want to travel by (*boat* / *plane*).

4 They miss their (*plane* / *train*).

5 They (*are* / *aren't*) always happy and excited.

6 *Feelings* can make you feel (*embarrassed* / *sad*).

7 A review

We usually use capital letters for titles of books, shows, films and plays.

Danny the Champion of the World
The Wizard of Oz

13 Write a review of a show / play / film you like.

- What's its name?
- What / Who is it about?
- What's the story?

- Where are the people?
- How does it make you feel?
- Why do you like it?

_____

_____

_____

_____

_____

_____

_____

_____

_____

_____

_____

By the sea 8
Outdoor activities

1 Read. Then write.

Across ➡

2 You wear riding __boots__ when you go horse-riding.

4 You do this under water: _____ diving.

6 You do this on fast rivers: _____ .

8 You need a _____ when you go kayaking.

Down ⬇

1 You need a fishing _____ to go fishing.

3 You need a _____ to go surfing.

5 When you go _____ jumping, you need a long rope.

7 You wear a life _____ when you go sailing.

2 Unscramble. Then write.

1 eskngroliln
s n o r k e l l i n g

2 kkaaigyn
_ _ _ _ _ _ _ _

3 nahg gligind
_ _ _ _   _ _ _ _ _ _ _

4 nrfaitg
_ _ _ _ _ _ _

5 sorhe-dirngi
_ _ _ _ _ _ - _ _ _ _ _ _

6 fsnrigu
_ _ _ _ _ _ _

8 Let's go fishing!

3 Read. Then circle.

1 Let's go (*snorkel / snorkelling*). I've got a (*snorkel / snorkelling*).

2 He doesn't (*like / liking*) rock climbing.

3 We're fond of (*raft / rafting*). I've got my own (*paddle / paddling*).

4 I'm (*crazy / terrified*) of scuba diving.

5 They're crazy about (*hang gliding / hang glide*).

6 I'm really (*fond / good*) at surfing. I've got (*surfboard / a surfboard*).

4 Complete the sentences with *of*, *about* or *with*.

1 I'm fond _____of_____ skateboarding.

2 Tom's bored _____ rollerblading.

3 We're scared _____ bungee jumping.

4 Sara is terrified _____ singing in front of people.

5 I'm crazy _____ water skiing.

6 They're fond _____ scuba diving.

5 Write sentences about you.

1 _____ (*fond*)

2 _____ (*crazy*)

3 _____ (*bored*)

4 _____ (*scared*)

5 _____ (*terrified*)

6 **Read. Then order the dialogue.**

[ ] Great idea! Have you got a surfboard?

[ ] I'm not fond of kayaking. What about surfing?

[ ] Hi, Ben. How are you?

[ ] Let's go horse-riding!

[1] Hi, Oli.

[ ] Sorry, I'm terrified of horses. What about kayaking?

[ ] I'm fine. What do you want to do today?

[ ] My dad has got one. Let's go and ask.

7 **Complete the conversation. Use the prompts.**

A: ¹Let's go kayaking! _____ (let's / kayaking)

B: ²_____ (I / terrified / kayaking)
What about fishing?

A: OK. ³_____ (you / have got / fishing rod / ?)

B: Yes, I've got two.

A: ⁴_____ (be / you / fond of / fishing / ?)

B: Yes! ⁵_____ (I / be / crazy about / fishing)

A: OK! Let's go!

8 **Look and read. Then write questions and answers.**

	Next Monday	Next weekend	Next year
Tom	do English test	go horse-riding	visit Argentina
Sara	play guitar	play video games	go to new school

1 What's Tom going to do next Monday?
He's going to do an English test.

2 What's Sara going to do next Monday?

_____

3 What's Tom going to do next weekend?

_____

4 What's Sara going to do next weekend?

She's going to play video games.

5 _____

He's going to visit Argentina.

6 _____

She's going to go to a new school.

9 **Complete the chart about you. Then write sentences.**

	Next Monday	Next weekend	Next year
Me	_____	_____	_____

1 I'm going to _____ .

2 _____

3 _____

10 **Read. Where are the children going to go?**

Alberto is _____.

Carla is _____.

Alberto's blog

I'm so excited! In August we're going to go to Wales. It's going to be the perfect holiday! I'm going to go sailing and fishing with my grandad and snorkelling with my sister. We're both very fond of it. I want to go hang gliding but my dad says I can't because I'm very young. I'm also going to go surfing. My cousin Pete is going to be there and we're going to go together. It's going to be so much fun!

Alberto 10, England

Carla's blog

I'm going to go to Scotland in June and I'm really happy! My cousins live there and we're going to do a lot of things together! We're going to go horse-riding. I love it because it makes me feel very relaxed. My sister's bored with horse-riding so she isn't going to come. We're all going to go rock climbing and hang gliding! There are a lot of beautiful places there so we are also going to go hiking. It's going to be fantastic!

Carla 10, South Africa

11 **Read again. Then write A (Alberto) or C (Carla).**

1 fishing $\boxed{A}$ **2** sailing $\boxed{}$

3 hang gliding $\boxed{}$ **4** hiking $\boxed{}$

5 horse-riding $\boxed{}$ **6** snorkelling $\boxed{}$

7 rock climbing $\boxed{}$ **8** surfing $\boxed{}$

8 A blog

Remember!

| ride | ➜ | rideing | ✗ | riding | ✓ |
| dive | ➜ | diveing | ✗ | diving | ✓ |

12 Imagine you are going to go on the perfect holiday. Write about it in your blog.

- Where are you going to go? When?

- What activities are you going to do?

- Who are you going to do them with?

- How do these activities make you feel?

_____ blog ✕

_____

_____

_____

_____

_____

_____

_____

_____

_____

_____